PRAISE FOR DOROTHY V

The poems of Dorothy Walters speak with the creative brilliance of Rumi, the passion of Mirabai, the humor of Hafiz, and the deep insight of John of the Cross – yet the voice is entirely her own. Her poems carry the delight and astonishment that come only from the most direct, personal experience of the sacred. They bypass theology and theory and lead us dancing into the presence of the Goddess Kundalini.

Ivan M. Granger, editor of *This Dance of Bliss: Ecstatic Poetry from Around the World*

Walter's poems are imbued with the fiery taste of the constantly dis-appearing sacred.

Eve Ensler, author of *The Vagina Monologues*

Dorothy Walters is too gracefully human to accept my calling her a saint; I will call her instead a prophetic visionary poet, who sits at the Banquet Table of Aloneness with so many friends like Hafiz, Rumi, Rilke, and Mary Oliver. On Dorothy's pathless path, we enter the grace of an inward alchemy, and her poems are drops of that alchemical nectar that transmutes loneliness into rapture. Yet these poems are deceptively conversational, as if, on a Sabbath afternoon, we've met a quite ordinary elder sitting on a park bench; and only later do our hearts burn, as we realize we were learning from an angel whose soul is pure fire.

Alfred LaMotte, author of *Savor Eternity One Moment At A Time*

Dorothy Walters' luminous poems are literal transmissions of the possible for every soul who braves the peaks and valleys of the Path Within. We are extraordinarily blessed to have them. Actually, one does not read these poems. They are taken in directly through the heart. Dorothy has delivered us to the gate of bliss and welcomes us home.

Claudia Helade, Ph.D., artist and transpersonal psychotherapist

Walters has the heart of a mystic, rooted in the ecstatic tradition where the divine overflows into daily life. Her poems invite us into this holy mystery, reading becomes an act of prayer itself.

Christine Valters Paintner, Ph.D., author of *The Soul of the Pilgrim*

BOOKS BY DOROTHY WALTERS

Some Kiss We Want: Poems Selected and New

Marrow of Flame: Poems of the Spiritual Journey

The Lay Lines of the Soul: Poems of Ecstasy and Ascension

A Cloth of Fine Gold: Poems of the Inner Journey

Penelope's Loom: Poems of Turning Matter into Spirit

Unmasking the Rose: A Record of a Kundalini Initiation

Moonlight on a Night Moth's Wing, art by Rashani Rea

Flannery O'Connor

I Hear My Sisters Saying: Poems of Twentieth Century Women, co-editor Carol Konek

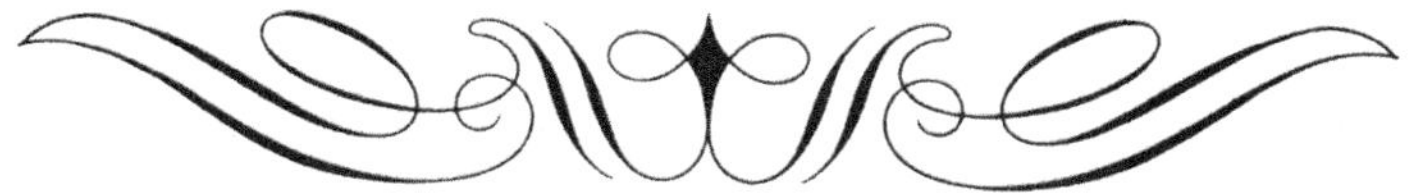

The Kundalini Poems

Reflections of Radiance and Joy

by

Dorothy Walters

For information contact Emergence Education Press,
PO Box 63767, Philadelphia, PA 19147.

ISBN-10: 0-9995658-2-6

ISBN-13: 978-0-9995658-2-7

Library of Congress Control Number: 2018961509

Published in the United States of America by:

Emergence Education Press
P.O. Box 63767
Philadelphia, PA 19147

www.EmergenceEducation.com

Cover Image: Caroline Maniere
Cover Design: Arinze Ikeli

For more on Dorothy Walter's work:
https://kundalinisplendor.blogspot.com/

Printed & bound in the United States of America

TABLE OF CONTENTS

Preface	i
Introduction	iii
Invocation to Kundalini	1
Seekers	2
Who I Am	4
Kundalini, The Life Force	5
The Divine Alchemy	7
What is it?	8
The Key Moment	9
Enlightenment	11
Sacred Emissaries	13
Where the Beauty Resides	15
Two Kinds of Intelligence	16
The Holy Temptress	19
The Inner Music	20
You	21
Like Light Playing Over Water	22
On Reading Kabir	23
These Honey Drops	24
Questions for Kabir	25
The Secret Lover	26
Snow	27
Buddha's Pronouncement	28
Second Coming	30
The Initiation	32

When	34
Eight Ways the Flower Opens	35
The Saints	38
Even if No One Accepts the Miracle	39
To the One Within	40
The Secret	42
The Transformed Human	43
A Tribute for Mary Oliver	45
Kissing the Hem of Mary Oliver: *Devotions*	47
Mary Oliver's Face	49
The Lost Seeker	50
The Blossoming	51
My Life Moves Forward	52
Dancers	54
The Savants	55
Yab/Yum, Shiva/Shakti	56
Yab/Yum as Ultimate	57
Wounded	58
When It's Over	60
All We Want	61
The Longing	62
The Awakening	63
When We Are Making Love	66
Sensitive Ears	67
Afterwards	68
Those Sanctified Ones	69
Deva Premal	70
The Ascent	71
How to Ascend	73

Holy Union	75
The Beloved Shares Her Secret	76
The Solitary Ecstatic	78
Seeds	79
Bodhidharma	81
What I Must Do	82
The Visitor	83
Sudden Turns	84
The One Kiss	86
Buddha's Flower	87
Always	88
In My House of Flesh	89
Oh, Seeker	91
The True Guide	92
No Entrance Fee	93
The Unseen Poet	95
Question	96
Tonight	98
The Ancient Saint Reflects	99
The Mythologized Saint Speaks	101
Blessing	103
The Awakened One's Dilemma	105
Kundalini, The Beloved Within	106
Kundalini Speaks	107
Singers	108
Whatever Else	110
Thinking Ahead	111
The Wedding Night	114
At the Temple Gates	115

Our Beginning 116
Climbers 118
Past Life 120
Nataraja 122
Sudden Insights 123
The Traveler 125
The Unrepentant 127
A Mandala 129
Poets 130
Advice for Going On 132
The Mirror 134
Cinderella: The Rebirth 135
Sleeping Beauty 136
Romeo and Juliet 138
Remembering Narcissus 140
Nada Brahma 141
Rilke in Glory 143
When I Return 145
Sanskrit Syllables 147
Sanskrit Chanted by a Swami 149
Dreamers Beneath the Quilts 150
The God Particle 151
Questions 153
A Stone, a Star 155
Transfiguration 157
Tricks up its Sleeves 158
Some Other Place 159
How It Will Happen 160
Drinking Song 161

The Transformation 162
Angels 164
When the Great Angel Came 165
Because 167
A Delicate Rapture 168
Who We Are 170
The Happening 171
The Initiation 173
The Transition 175
About the Author 177

PREFACE

THE GODDESS KUNDALINI

Of all the goddesses, Kundalini is the greatest. She is the goddess of goddesses, the life force itself, the ultimate quintessence of the divine feminine. She runs through every living creature and keeps them alive and sensitive to the ultimate connection with that which is real. She is indeed everywhere and nowhere, within and without. When she visits, she grants us profound ecstasy or possibly its opposite, when our energies fall out of alignment.

She is the unseen essence behind every representation of the goddess, whether as archetype or human embodiment. She is known by many names: the Great Mother in the Mediterranean in early times, the Shekinah among the Jews, Shakti and various other goddesses in yogic lore. Some feel she is the Holy Spirit of Christian tradition. She is known in every society and culture throughout the world and in every era. She is the inspiration behind all creative expression, whether in art, poetry, or song. She keeps us alive and makes us human. She is, ultimately who we are, for we are spun from her essence in our beginning.

Kundalini awakened is the gift of the soul's journey, the jewel hiding in the within, the ultimate prize that returns us to our original nature.

She may arrive swiftly, sometimes without any apparent

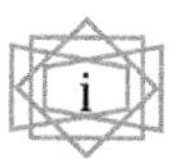

background or preparation on our part, or she may unfold quietly, slowly, after years of devotional practice. The taste of her bliss will vary from person to person and again within the same person from day to day. Her presence is honored by every known culture since humans appeared on this planet.

Kundalini is the great mystery in which we all are embedded. She is not a thought form nor an idea. She can be known only at the feeling level, for she is the ultimate connection with Source. She is the raw, perfect, longed for experience that unites our awareness (finally) to what we are. At last, we encounter our true identity and our purpose and mission on this planet, as we move together into the next stage of our human evolution.

This volume is dedicated to Kundalini, the enigmatic bestower of inner wisdom and joy, and to the following goddesses and gods in my life:

Andrew Harvey
Patricia Lay Dorsey
Craig Johnson
Philip Overbaugh
Claudia Helade
Gloria Coelho
Karen Lester
Diane Knoll
Kathy Fowler
Dawn Hartman
Stephanie Marohn
Gina Barnett
Jacqueline Arnold
Ed Arnold
Nancy Stetson
Sally Terwillinger
Peggy Wrenn
Mirabai Starr
Ivan Granger
Lawrence Edwards
Helen Purdun
Amy Edelstein
Jeff Carreira

INTRODUCTION

In 1981 I was living in Kansas, teaching English and Women's Studies at a state university. On the whole, my life was good. I had discovered the Great Mother and felt her power within. I had dabbled in certain esoteric realms such as Caballa, alchemy, the Tarot, and ESP. I had read and reflected on many stimulating writers, such as Jung and Eliade, and was actively involved in the feminist movement that was just stirring in the U.S. and elsewhere. I was in a long-term relationship with a compatible partner. I had no inkling that something was about to happen that would change my life forever.

What occurred is called "spontaneous Kundalini awakening." I knew almost nothing about this mysterious energy. I had never meditated nor done Yoga, *tai chi*, or any other energy practices. I had never even had a massage. I was someone who lived more in my head than in my body.

At that time, Kundalini was still virtually unheard of in the West. There were no workshops and scarcely any books on the topic. Indeed, I knew no one who had even heard of this phenomenon. Today Kundalini is virtually a buzzword, but such was not the case in those days. Yoga studios now abound on virtually every corner, and classes in energetic awakening are readily available. Nothing of the sort was part of the mass culture in that era and certainly not where I was living.

Here is how it happened:

To begin with, I was in psychological turmoil. The relationship

that had seemed to be so solid appeared to be breaking up. I was devastated. Mental trauma was ripping a hole my psyche, my sense of self. It is said that when major crisis occurs, something can appear to fill in the gap, the vacancy that has been created. And so it did.

By some "coincidence" I happened to be reading a book at that time which briefly alluded to Kundalini, but did not explain in detail what it was nor offer any techniques for experiencing it. It talked of a "serpent" resting at the base of the spine that could be raised up through various "chakras" (whatever those might be) to the top of the head, where the crown would open "like a many petaled lotus" unfolding. This effect would only come after many years of devoted practice including many spiritual rituals and rigid discipline. The aspirant was warned that this could be a most dangerous undertaking and thus should be attempted only under the supervision of an experienced teacher.

For some reason I was intrigued by this strange notion (Kundalini, the life force) and decided to give it a try. So I meditated on an illustration in this book of the famous image called "yab/yum," the god and goddess in close embrace, as well of another of St. Teresa of Avila in a state of ecstatic trance. I seemed to project my energies into male and female in turn, and then the two of them in union. Then I breathed as deeply as I could and focused on bringing the energies upward. After I had done this for a very few minutes, my energies broke loose and literally shot into my head. I entered what I later learned to call a state of rapture, as indescribably ecstatic pulsations occurred in my crown. I realized that I had uncovered the reality that is the basis of the cosmos, the vast incomprehensible essence of which each of us is a minute part, and that we partake of this source but only in the way a cell is a tiny constituent of our

body, but not the whole.

I longed for guidance, but there was simply no one to advise me or even to confide in. There were no Kundalini teachers or yoga studios near me at that time. Thus I maintained a silence for some fifteen years. I became a "solitary practitioner," with recurring episodes of ecstasy and pain, as the energies sought to bring balance into my system. Even much later when I consulted so called energy 'experts' about my continuing bliss states, I was given such responses as "If you are lucky, you will get over this" and (from a renowned *qigong* teacher) "No, the literature explains that the energies can be hot, cold, or electric" but nothing is said about what you describe.

And so I became a solitary ecstatic, someone who underwent periods of deep rapture day after day for weeks and even years, these interspersed with times of challenge and pain as my body strove to assimilate these new energies into my system.

Since I had no one to talk to, I kept a journal of my inner adventure, and, ultimately, fashioned and published a book ("Unmasking the Rose") on my initiation into this remarkable state of consciousness.

Then in the mid-nineties when I had moved to San Francisco, I met Andrew Harvey, renowned spiritual teacher. He listened attentively to my story and urged me to write poetry reflecting the stages of my spiritual transformation. And so I did. I published a selection of poems from the four books I had previously written (*Some Kiss We Want: Poems Selected and New*) in 2016.

I continued to write and the more poems I wrote focusing on the spiritual path, the easier the practice became. The present volume is drawn from those verses composed over the last

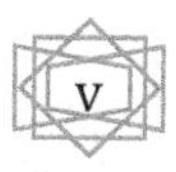

eighteen months as the creative flow became more and more vibrant and the text easier to receive, for these are poems that have been "received" from an unknown source, rather than constructions of my own.

For me, Kundalini is the face of the Beloved Within, who continues to announce Her presence from time to time even after many years with bliss itself as the marker. These exquisite moments bring us ever closer to the ultimate, to Divine Reality and the Love that permeates the universe. I agree with the many now proclaiming that we are currently in a time of the evolution of human consciousness as we all progress to becoming divine humans.

Kundalini is the sacred trigger, the designated mechanism by which this is happening. It awakens us to the truth of our own nature and reveals the holy connection between self and vast Other.

As I write this it is the year 2018. Recently I celebrated my ninetieth birthday, and I feel blessed to have been allowed to move this far on my journey of inner awakening and capturing in poetry some aspects of that experience.

Joseph Campbell says that the final stage of the life journey is bringing the gift back home. This is my gift to all who are open to receive. It is my hope that it will light the way and give encouragement to the many who are currently undertaking their own soul voyages into the universe of cosmic love at this time.

Namaste and Blessings to all.

Dorothy Walters

July 2018

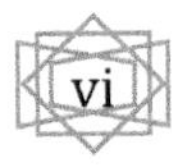

INVOCATION TO KUNDALINI

Oh, Mother of all mothers,
Goddess of all the gods,
hold us tightly
in your embrace.

Let what was unknown
become known,
what was hidden
come into light.

This is our time
to come together,
to be infused
with your divine energies,
to know that we are
yours, eternally,
even now
as we move ahead
into the vast unknown,
drown us in the sea of love.

SEEKERS

What you seek was seeking you.
Rumi

How is it
that when I was
looking for You,
You were seeking me also?

Silently You watched and waited.
Sometimes gave me
a brief glimpse
or taste
of who You were,
like a shy deer in the forest
that vanishes when
you turn to look.

And so I roamed,
looking here and there,
gazing at the hieroglyphs on trees
or peering into the throats of flowers for secret revelations,
listening to the waves
pounding the shore for messages,
examining books and stars,
seeking essence.

Finally I gave up my searching,
surrendered my deep desire
to stillness.
And then You gave me a kiss
that lasted forever.

WHO I AM

I am neither Muslim
nor Jew.
Buddha does not tie my feet.
I gave up being a Protestant long ago.

Too wild for the Taoists,
too tame for the Tantrics,
neither breathing
nor transfixed
nor saying magic words.

Yet for years I yearned,
followed formulas in ancient texts,
listened to the saints
and philosophers
seeking wisdom.

Finally I gave up searching,
stood very still
and fell
into who I am.

KUNDALINI, THE LIFE FORCE

What you must know
is this:
it will not come
as a thought
or a concept
or an experiment
in a laboratory.

It will not be an extension
of all that has been proved
by wise men
in tomes and bound volumes
for centuries before.

It will happen
within what you call
your body.
You will not know
where your flesh ends
and a feeling comes that is
both outside and inside,
a realization arriving
as an experience,
a happening
you have no words to describe.

Of course, you can try.
You can speak of it
as rapture, as ecstasy,
as a flowing field of bliss.

But once it happens,
you will recognize it
as that which unites all
and of which you are an
indivisible part.

Drop to ocean,
cells to body,
the nameless you to
Love.

THE DIVINE ALCHEMY

The heavenly kilns
are waiting to receive us,
to shape us into a new configuration
until every nerve and fiber
is restrung.

Angels are posted
along the way to guide us,
but we must attend.

We must be refined in the
fires of love
again and again
until all dross is taken
and we are left as the naked flame
of that which we are,
the being connected
to the All.

The nugget to be carried in God's pocket,
the jewel in hiding
to be discovered
at last.

Kundalini is the goddess
in charge.

What Is It?

It has to do
with love.

It has to do with energy.

It has to do with the God force energy
that runs through everything.

It is how we feel
when we are finally connected.

It is God
moving through your body.

It is the Beloved making love
with you from within,
even when you are not
expecting it.

It is you
coming home to yourself
at last.

THE KEY MOMENT

After the key moment,
you will not be the same.
At first
you will feel like a ghost
returning from another realm
with a message
that no one wants to hear.

Or perhaps the one living being
walking about in a city of
the dead.

The world and all that is in it
is suddenly very beautiful
and you know that it and you
are one.

If you try to tell someone
what has happened,
they will look uneasy
and change the subject.
Or maybe suggest
that you should call 911,
check yourself in.

You learn to be silent,
pretend to be like them.

They are all very busy, buying the latest gadgets,
showing off their new clothes,
watching the game or the
commercials on T. V.

If they wish to be good,
they take the children to church,
but don't listen when the minister
rambles on telling them how they should live.
They secretly look at their cell phones,
watch the athletic events in progress,
check their investments.

Each day you listen
to celestial music,
but nobody else can hear.
You know that angels
are floating overhead
on golden clouds,
but no one wishes to look up.

You learn to be silent,
never reveal what has happened,
who you are.
You live in your own secret world
where your only companion
is God.

ENLIGHTENMENT

After you are enlightened
it is hard to hold steady.

Blinded by light
so strong
that the mind is stunned
and the world around dissolves.

You have been given a vision of
that which you may not care to know.

Who wants to be told
that they do not exist?
That they are as raindrop
to sea water,
corpuscle to self.

Possessor of a secret that you can't explain
and that you dare not share.

Yet overall you welcomed it,
it was love, love, love,
and you and the lover as one.

A memory that remains ever,
returns in subtler form,

guiding you through
as you plod ahead
on this unexpected life you
are called to live.

SACRED EMISSARIES

Some of us have been
priests and priestesses
since time began.

In Egypt we served in the
pyramids,
we cast the spells
mixed the potions,
to bring healing
to the people,
food for the land.

In Greece we roved
the mountains,
thyrsus in hand,
uniting with nature,
the oracle speaking words
with earth's tongue.

As shamans we flew
high into the heavens
to bring down light
and secret wisdom.
The gods were merciful,
shared the secrets,
yet many died on the way.

But it was there,
in sacred East,
that we truly found our path
to union with the gods.
They and we were one,
our ceremonies of fire and chant
calling them down
and we became other.

We still inhabit this present
world that does not care.
We are called by different names,
live hidden,
are seldom seen.
Mountains, forests,
running streams—
if you look,
you will find us there.
If you listen,
you will hear us speak.

Sometimes we will arrive suddenly,
fill your bodies
with a joy you cannot name.

Where the Beauty Resides

Will someone please tell me
what day it is,
what time?

More and more I keep on living
in that place that has no date,
and no measuring instruments for time.

And then when I return
to that other world,
the one they call "real"
with its clocks and calendars,
its appointment books and meetings,
I come blinking and dazed,
wonder what all the confusion is about,
yearn to hurry back to that other realm
where the beauty resides.

TWO KINDS OF INTELLIGENCE

There are two kinds of intelligence.
Rumi

One is the sort
we acquire in school,
where we memorize,
dissect, discard
what our feelings tell us
about the direction
our hearts wish to go.

Thus we develop skills
that command
a high price
in the market.
We marry our computers,
or learn to take the stuff
of this world apart,
ever finding new components
to add to an already existing
array of proficiencies.

We thus are certain
that we know what we know,
and never have to think
about other possibilities,

sovereigns of our chosen
kingdoms.

We often become famous,
win prizes,
acclaimed for our discoveries
that make us ever more
marketable.

The other kind of knowledge.
opens us to the secrets of
plants and paintings
and waves tossing against the shore.
We marry certain trees
and betroth ourselves
to flowers.
Evening clouds
take us aback
with their shifting
array of colors,
purple and subtle orange.
It envelops us
in a kind of awe at concerts,
where we allow ourselves
to be ravished
by sound, frequencies arriving
in nuanced order
to echo deep within.

This kind of knowing
commands love,

a caring for those
who cross our path,
a way of connecting with
others, even those
we have never seen.

This way is not marketable.

It constantly turns the base metal
of our lives into gold.

THE HOLY TEMPTRESS

Her primary attribute
is that she is unpredictable.

Fickle suitor,
sometimes She enters
by cheek or brow,
sometimes by hands,
and again in the chakras,
high or low.

She is like a lover
who slips up behind
and gives you a kiss
on your neck
before you know who is
there.

Sometimes
She is waiting
when you wake up
ready to enfold you
in Her arms.

Always when She beckons
you come.

THE INNER MUSIC

If you have only learned the signs and colors,
you have missed it.

If you memorize the petals
and the aspects of the body,
even the animals,
that is not where it is.

The charts and classifications,
they will lead you astray,
no wedding day arrives.

Only the inner kiss
of the beloved
will take you there.

Shiva/Shakti,
embracing inside,
constant happening,
love play within,
music of desire,
only this,
only this.

YOU

I never know
just when you are going
to come.

Sometimes it is as though
you are there, always,
hidden behind the couch,
waiting to spring.

Or else curled behind my ear,
ready to burst
into a *gloria.*

Sometimes you are merely
a scattering of rocks
tinted by the
sun,
or a tree
gently swaying,
whisper of leaves.

Somehow I think you never really leave,
just hide inside your
invisibility cape
and then I look around
and see nothing
but you everywhere.

LIKE LIGHT PLAYING OVER WATER

Happening again.
She has come.
Even sitting here,
receiving these words,
I feel Her stirring within.

I do not know where
She comes from,
why She visits,
how She travels.

Now sweetness moves
from feet to temples,
then back again.

Each time it is
like a lover's kiss
after long absence.

Why am I trying to
make sentences
about this?

The answer
is in the breath.

ON READING KABIR AS TRANSLATED BY ANDREW HARVEY

Kabir, you have made me drunk
with your verses and I have lost
all my bearings.

Up, down, night, day, real, fantasy—
now all the same to me.

But I am not complaining.
I like this being tipsy.
Whatever you do,
don't make me get
sober again.

THESE HONEY DROPS

Kabir, Kabir,
when I read your poems
I melt into the earth.
Or if I stay upright,
a certain sun lights
all my pores
and I become a vague outline
of Desire.

Tell me, who places these honey drops
on your tongue?
who sends you these sweetmeats
made of words . . .

All I want
is more.

QUESTIONS FOR KABIR

How is it that I write these poems
all morning,
then find these stunning verses from the Master
with the same themes all afternoon?

There is a well of truth
from which we all must drink.
Some take deep draughts,
others a few sips now and then.

Oddly the thoughts they present
often resemble each other
yet in different language,
his luminous,
mine trying to capture
invisible light.

THE SECRET LOVER

Stroke of feather on flesh, not flesh.

Touch of silk on body, not body.

Light playing over water, not water.

Each movement, breath, ananda.

SNOW

Snow on the high peaks.

Mist in the valley.

Birdsong dissolving in
darkness.

I alone by the fire
with my invisible.

BUDDHA'S PRONOUNCEMENT

Buddha, I don't understand
your message.
Old age, sickness and death--
indeed they come to us all
and many of my friends
have already gone,
having succumbed early and late
to each of these.

What are you trying
to tell us?
I think I am hearing it
wrong.
Should we not care about these?
Show compassion
when others fall?
Should we not be honest
and confess
that when our time arrives,
we will likewise go
through the final stages
and not be sure why?

If nothing in this life script
matters,
how does life itself count?
Were we sent here

for a purpose?
And must we taste
old age, sickness
and death
many times over
as part of the bargain?

Buddha, you leave out
holy rapture,
union itself the goal
and end.

I know I cannot
think my way to God.

I must find
someone ancient and wise
sitting under
a tree
to explain such things,
set me straight.

SECOND COMING

When You first arrived
you were a tornado
that tore my mind to shreds.
All of the edifices that I had made
to tell me who I was
crumbled and fell,
my thoughts and notions
obliterated,
my theories destroyed
to dust.
Sentences were not possible,
paragraphs beyond my grasp.

All I had left was this
honey scent
You left behind,
the blinding nectar
of Your love.
I drank and drank of this
sweet wine,
and forgot all other concerns.

Gradually something has rebuilt
the ruins of what
was left behind,
shards and remnants
now retrieved to make a new habitation.

I now command a retinue
of ideas and rhetoric,
find pleasure in thought and theory,
and only sometimes seek your presence
in between.

When will you come again?
Will you enter this new structure,
find me once more unprepared,
and again abducted after I have shed my mental
coverings,
once more blasted
to become I know not what?

THE INITIATION FOR GENEVIEVE

When it happens,
you will not know what it is.
You will go trembling and afraid
into the arms of an unseen lover,
one who will hold you tightly
in a close embrace.

You will sigh
and give in,
relinquish all control.
You will let it have its way with you.
You will not know if
it is male or female,
but you will not care.

The rapture will extend
until night itself
groans in joy.

In the morning you
will realize
that you have just made
love with God,

that this is what you
have always longed for,
that you yourself
are the god within.

WHEN

When your body opens
you will be a flower
swallowing sun,
earth pierced by rain.

Child at mother's breast,
lover entering and being entered.

Pulsation of joy.

Kiss of heaven.

EIGHT WAYS THE FLOWER OPENS

You are entered
and ravished
by something
you cannot see.
Your body pulses
in pleasure and joy.
Finally you lie
on the earth, arms outstretched,
and say, "Here I am, take me,
I am yours."

You move slowly,
blossom gently kissed by rain.
You struggle cautiously
up the mountain,
wondering why
you are doing this,
if you should go on.
Someone has said
there are unicorns
and hanging gardens
up ahead
and so you
continue to climb.

You find teachers
who dispense universal wisdom.

They lead you,
give you things to do.
Sometimes you touch
their hems in gratitude,
receive their blessings.

You scour old texts,
examine ancient scrolls.
You look carefully,
certain that the secret is there,
the guide to the hidden treasure
waiting to be found.

You are a skeptic and see
that the others are bewitched
by a comforting trance,
myths to sustain
in an uncertain world.
You remain alone in your tower of truth,
and know that you are braver, wiser,
more enlightened than the rest,
for you have seen through
to where nothing is.
Then one day something happens,
some kind of light
dispels the darkness
and everything changes
forever.

You cast aside all instruction,
do it your chosen way,
paintings and dancing,
music and poems,

trees that sing to you,
waves pummeling the shore.
Something unknown
directs your movements,
you are led by an invisible guide
into the realms of the subtle raptures.
Finally a voice speaks to you within.
You pause and listen.

You arrive somewhere,
know that this is the place
you have been seeking
for so long.
Your crown opens and
you scan the landscape
with new eyes.
Everything dazzles
illumined by an inner sun,
you know that you are nothing,
all is one.

People call you a saint
or a savior.
You wonder how this
could be.
You return
to the foot of the mountain,
again struggle upward
over the rubble and scree,
pilgrim among pilgrims,
help others
as best you can.

THE SAINTS

These were not like us,
these ancient ones.
They lived in caves,
ate grass,
lashed themselves to poles
and stood one legged
in the sky.

Some flew up to the church ceiling,
then wondered how they
would get down.
Others healed by allowing those in need
to touch their hem,
receive grace through the eyes.

Yet we survive.
The rapture comes and we receive.
Who can tell how sweet and soft it is,
or tumultuous like a storm,
pulsation of bliss.

We have no guide
or explanation.
Only the wonder
of the real.
Merely the kiss
of that which is.

EVEN IF NO ONE ACCEPTS THE MIRACLE

This title was inspired by Mary Oliver

Believe it.
These things happen.
To you, to me,
to every one of us
every day.

That squirrel that lingered
in the grass so long and gazed
into your eyes as you went by.
That tree with its
marvelous curlicues called bark.
Those fallen leaves forming
a radiant tapestry on the ground,
violet, gold, soft scarlet,
each in its appointed place.

Are these not miracles?
Are they not perfect?
Isn't it a miracle
to be alive,
to hear this music and
move in joy about the room,
to take in each breath
one after another,
even if no one
taught you how?

TO THE ONE WITHIN

I have nothing.
Not even a robe
or a mark on my brow.
I do not wish to wear jeweled garments
and wear a halo around my head
and talk to large gatherings of people
to tell them what to think
or get smashed in crowds
at festivals and celebrations.
No longer able to do floor yoga,
instead I stand and move gently
here and there.
I bring no incense or offerings
of fruit or flowers,
kiss no feet.
My temple is silence.

Yet at times
I know You are there.
When You come I forget all else,
what the others think or do.
It does not matter
if I am clothed or naked,
fed or hungry.
My moves are subtle,
yet they bring much bliss.

Others would not believe
even if I told.

These meetings are secret.
Something between the
two of us.
Union that some
are looking for
and often have not found.

Om shanti, om shanti, om shanti, om

THE SECRET

A hundred scholars
could search the texts
and never find the meanings.

Yogis can turn themselves into pretzels,
become limber as serpents
and still not know the secret.

I think such knowings come from bargains
struck long ago
in a place that has no name.

Formulas were sewn
into your spine and skull,
ready to be found.

No one truly understands
how all this happens,
how some are chosen,
some not.

This is a process
that some call grace.

You must listen carefully
to hear
when your name is called.

THE TRANSFORMED HUMAN

The cabalists called it "Adam Kadmon"
and followed strange practices
to achieve their goal.
The alchemists strove to turn
the base metal of the species into gold,
always in secret,
away from censoring eyes.
Teilhard de Chardin said it would happen
at the Omega Point, the place
where heaven and earth meet.
Aurobindo spoke of the Divine Human,
something in the making,
and we hold our own notions
of the New Person now being born.
The Transformed Human.

Who is this being
so long sought, so fervently desired?
Are we ourselves being cast into a new mold,
a better, more luminous,
more transcendent version of ourselves?

Will our refashioned nerves and renewed senses
carry us to an unknown way of perceiving
and acting,
a more peaceful and caring

way of relating to ourselves
and the world?

Will we now be more closely connected
to the unseen Divine?

What is the power propelling
such transfiguration?
Is it cosmic energy, predestination,
benevolent beings from elsewhere,
places far removed?
Unseen divinities shaping
our course,
gods who cherish us,
leading us on?

Some say it is an inevitable process
of nature, where simpler systems
always combine into higher
formulations of themselves.
Some feel it is Kundalini,
life force entering and animating all.

Some call it a field of Love,
pulsating god source that holds all of us
in its embrace,
shows us the way.

A TRIBUTE FOR MARY OLIVER

She came among us
like a wild creature
fresh from the forest,
wearing a tunic of green,
wreath of flowers in her hair.

Orpheus returned,
she sang to us of mysteries
long lost,
secrets of the animals
and trees,
how these were
our ancestors,
beloved precursors
of our souls.

Bears, rabbits, garden snakes,
small bodies of water,
even spiders--
all received her blessing,
all part of the oneness that is.

We listened in awe
to her sacred melodies,
in trance and yearning
for what we had forgotten,

our lost songs of spirit,
ceremonies of connection,
the place where we began.

Kissing the Hem of Mary Oliver: Devotions

Here she is, I am holding her
in my hands.
A new and weighty book,
the record of her life,
each beauty (a leaf, a star)
tumbling forth
one after another,
her memorial,
her memory book,
her journey of
so many years.

She loved, was one with
nature itself,
the birds, the ponds,
the bears in the trees.
Even the insects
and snakes,
nothing was excluded,
she was the original
nature mystic
from ages past,
a goddess or queen
from some other world,

returned to ours
to give us
new eyes to see,
new ways to connect
with what so many had
forgotten
amidst the concrete
and clatter
of this wherever we have made,
glimpses of the place
where our
Mother lived,
the realm from which we came.

MARY OLIVER'S FACE

Gaze on this portrait
and what you will see
is someone who has
grown old and wise,
who sees with ineluctable
clarity the inner truth of things
and knows who she is.

She carries her age well,
allowing each wrinkle
and shadow
to define her essence:
knowing, resolute,
yet with a wry pixie smile
that says
she is taking the world
and her life
with a grain of salt,
knows that not this
nor any poem
can be the final answer,
now waiting with poise
and grace to receive
the next unfolding.

THE LOST SEEKER

Oh, where is my robe?
I have looked everywhere
and I cannot find it.

When I meet others
wearing their robes and beads,
my heart clutches in envy.
They know how to chant mantras
and sing kirtan,
ways to fall into the secret
rapture.
They turn about
on their jeweled sandals,
each movement a blessing.

I have neither bindu nor robe,
no scepter or crown,
only the sacred presence within.
Only the kisses that She
and I know together
when "naked to naked goes."

The phrase "naked to naked goes" is from Yeats. It refers to the moment when the pure spirit encounters beloved source.

THE BLOSSOMING

If I could step out of my body, I would break into blossom.
James Wright

Yes, you and I have done this,
remember the times
when the stars have spoken to us
and rainbows flung themselves
across the spume and the heaving
waves.

Or perhaps it was when
someone special
entered the room,
or when the Mahler
entered our bodies,
and all our chakras
opened at once.

And if you have had
the true awakening
you will indeed float
from your body
and find your lost home
within and everywhere without
as a lotus blooms above
your head.

My Life Moves Forward

My life moves forward
in ever widening circles.
Rilke

My life moves forward in a spiral,
now ascending seeking its star,
now circling earthward
to regions unknown.

Like a funnel of water
crossing the sea
it flows upward and again descends.
Yet always moving ahead,
ongoing progression of minutes
like a hawk rounding the heavens
before a swift plummeting downward
to seize its target
and claim it as its own.

When will I spiral upward
into final vastness,
unravel the message
in the clouds,
find the one who awaits
to seize me in joy?

For the Beloved Within
Neither male nor female.

Neither enfleshed
nor without form.

Neither nameless
nor known.

You come from elsewhere,
a place of joy
not revealed
to us below.

Often you arrive
without warning
in unexpected circumstances.

I call you
my Beloved.

I know you
by your kisses.

My only prayer:
"Do not leave me
here alone once more."

DANCERS

All around we are seeing
a world in ruins.
I do not need to tell you
all the things going wrong.

Yet there is another world
rising and unfolding
within and without.
The frequencies are changing.

People are feeling it everywhere
and becoming
that which is more than
they have been.

I know.
I have met them again
and again and
they are beautiful.

They are dancing
amidst the rubble,
night and day,
they are ascending,
they are making love
with the unseen.

THE SAVANTS

They are always talking
about this and that,
looking things up in
dictionaries and encyclopedias,
quoting the authorities.

They have theories
and philosophies
that get bandied about
and debated,
presented at meetings,
published in journals.

Sometimes they occupy
positions in well known universities,
travel across the globe
to present their conclusions
at prestigious venues.

Have they ever known
the one true moment?
Have they ever suddenly
shuddered in delight
from an unknown cause?
Have they ever felt the single kiss
that tells them they are alive?

YAB/YUM, SHIVA/SHAKTI

They will tell you
that this image depicts
wisdom and compassion joined,
a lovely explanation,
but look again.

The god embraces himself
as female,
and she in turn becomes
who he is.

They have been locked
together like this
for countless eons,
they will continue into eternity.

They are telling us
that we must love
all parts of who we are,
that which is male,
that which is female,
just as these exist in all the cosmos
in union forever
as lovers, as one.

YAB/YUM AS ULTIMATE

Gaze on this image.
Let it resonate
in your body.
Become the female,
become the male,
become the two of them
united forever.
This is who you are.
You are all the opposites
combined.
The divine female/
the divine male
light/dark
earth/sky
motion/stillness
separation/unity
manifestation/source
bodiless/embodied
wisdom/compassion
god/human.

Contemplate this image
and know truth.

Let your body
become a sounding board
of the divine.

WOUNDED

God found me
and wounded me
into being.
I was safe before,
waiting for nothing
and then something
took me
into a strange place,
where I could not find God
nor hear my own voice.

"Who are these others?"
I asked, me without words.
"Why am I here?"
I wondered.
Silence surrounded me,
resonated in my cells.

Finally I found music.
Finally I found trees.
Even words
escaped from my mouth.

Then one day
I found out who I was.
Something called love
entered my body.

Now I look around
and see myself everywhere,
shining, beautiful,
complete.

WHEN IT'S OVER

When it's over, I want to say: all my life I
was a bride married to amazement.
Mary Oliver

And in turn I want to say I was married
to something called mystery. She never
explained herself
or showed her naked face,
but kept her veils securely
fastened over her countenance
as if she came from a country
whose laws demanded such modesty.

Yet often I felt
her bodiless body
mingle with mine,
her kisses
arrive in unexplained places.

Often I wondered
who she was,
where she came from
what her purpose.

At times I almost glimpsed
her secret origins.
Finally I no longer questioned
who she was,
why we were wedded as one,
but held her close
and silently exulted
in our secret love play.

All We Want

We claim to know things
but all that we know
can be written on a fingernail.

Sages and savants
issue their proclamations,
but we move always
through a dark cloud
with an uncertain light at the center.

The center is what we call God.
We keep on circling and circling
yet we never arrive
at that final point.

But we know
that we move ever closer
to that place of mystery,
even if we cannot locate it
with precision.

But when the Beloved arrives
we no longer care
who wins the arguments,
whose theory is correct.
All we want is the one embrace
that tells us who we are.

THE LONGING

We long for a *Shangri La* of the soul,
a place where those gather
who went through the portal,
flung themselves into the fire,
and became beacons of light.

We want to hear words
from the lips
of the wise ones,
those who will open us,
give us messages
from unknown realms.

We wish to hear music
that will fill our bodies
with light,
to ascend to the regions
where spirit prevails
and we become beauty.

When will our transfiguration occur?
When will the ones from elsewhere
claim us,
carry us over the worlds
to that place we ache for,
which we once knew
as home?

THE AWAKENING

No one can explain to me
how this happened.
One day a jewel opened
in my head.
Its rays went forth,
turning my body into light
as it moved.

First I meditated on an image,
the great god who dances
to keep the world alive.
Then it was the one with a flute,
seducing all who listen.

After that it was sacred postures,
each a stance of rapture,
joy racing through my veins.

Next it was music,
divine supplication
of the ears.
And mantras repeated
as I listened,
Om Namah Shivaya
Om bhur bhuva swaha
Om Om Om

Sacred syllables resonating
every corpuscle and cell.

Then I bought a *thangka*
and placed it on my wall.
Each morning I bowed
to Buddha,
felt ecstasy flow in my head,
my circling blood.
Each time
a new teacher within,
always from a different place
with another instruction.

And always music,
kirtan, Brahms, Krishna Das,
too rich to imagine.

The bliss waves
grew ever more subtle,
more refined.
Slightly moving fingers,
gentle movements
of the eyes
enough to rouse the
indescribable joy.

Hands circling around
my body,
aura stroked in rapture,
each time a miracle,

ecstasy more delicate,
more refined.

Now even a whiff of
frankincense and myrrh enough
to summon *ananda*,
the field of bliss.

I am becoming a new arrangement
of who I have been.
I am being readied
to move onward in my life,
to ascend into a higher frequency
along with the throngs of us
who are also preparing
across our world.

This is the omega point,
the alchemic gold achieved.
We are all gripped by a love
who holds us
as we go through.

When We Are Making Love

Your god is male,
mine female.
But what difference
does it make?

When we are making love
with the invisible
gender does not matter.

All we know is the embrace
of the unnamed unfathomable
Other,
the One who finds us
in the night.

SENSITIVE EARS

The elderly and the infirm--
they have to be careful
or the traffic will run over them.

Often they are the ones
who carry the secret
in their vest pockets
but the others
don't stop long enough
to listen.

There are books
that describe such matters
but these hurriers don't read.

Beautiful music is playing,
but they don't care to hear it.
They prefer the din of the avenue,
the roar of the market floors.

Those with sensitive ears
know what I am talking about.
They live in quiet dwellings.
Often they wear worn clothes
and walk with a shuffle.
Yet they are the ones
who have found the treasure.

Afterwards

Afterwards, we become instruments
tuned to a finer register of being.

We hear music
that was never sung,
craft words of wisdom that we do not
comprehend,
enter fields of light beyond understanding
and speak with tongues
of flame.

Now we are the servants
of an unknown master.

Streams of joy
flow through,
echoes of love
consume us.

We become moving figures of becoming,
always rising to a higher vibration,
ever evolving into more and more subtle
reflections of grace.

THOSE SANCTIFIED ONES

What did they do,
those sanctified ones
of earlier days,
with their billowing clothes
and their curious hats,
married to God?

How did they react when they
felt that Other stirring in
their loins, arousing
their flesh
in unexpected places?

Did they call it the demon
and do penance,
bread and water,
prayers repeated endlessly?

Or did they welcome
the unknown suitor,
allow rapture to enter
and fill them with joy,
Teresa in her ecstasy,
the angel thrusting its lance
into her heart?

DEVA PREMAL

Listening to this hidden goddess sing,
I forget who I am,
for I am she.
I move my clasped hands
above my head
to awaken
the sweet centers within.

She rises from the scent
of the blossom
where she resides.

Now it is time to move,
the rhythms of the body
matching the cadence
of the music.

She is honey nectar
and I drink shamelessly,
a hummingbird's tongue
thrusting into a flower.

My body knows how to listen,
where to go.

My body is this, this
flowing light.

THE ASCENT

Always there is a new challenge, a fresh discovery.
Nothing ever remains the same.
Dorothy

We are all climbing up the mountain
but we are doing it in different ways.

Some are using pickaxes and ropes,
often swinging out into space
in daredevil ways.

Others of us are scrambling
over rocks and debris,
progress steady but slow.

The runners are ascending
as quickly as they can.
They like the fast lane
but often have to stop to catch
their breath.

The invisible helpers
(called angels) are moving alongside
to tend to the wounded and fallen,
to help them move ahead.
When these are embodied,
they are called bodhisattvas.

Near the top are those
who have almost arrived
and keep shouting encouragement
to those struggling below:
"Keep on, you can do it,
don't give up now."

Together we move upward,
knowing that something important
awaits us up ahead.
No one knows exactly
what that is,
but we know it is our destiny
that will embrace us
when we arrive,
tell us that at last
we have found our true selves,
what we have been seeking
for so long.

How to Ascend

If you want to ascend this mountain,
you must throw away
everything you have carried
to sustain you thus far.

No maps, no compasses,
no neatly packed lunches
and flasks of refreshing drinks.

You must be willing
to climb alone
into unmarked regions,
across valleys and steep hills,
over rocks and boulders,
scree and ice.

At times you will think
you cannot go on,
that you will perish
of exhaustion,
of feelings of abandonment.

A voice will say, "Continue"
and you will summon your strength,
even if your boots are torn
and your body cries out
for rest.

When you finally arrive there,
you will be blinded by light
and ravished by love.

You will wonder if this is what you came for,
the prize you were seeking.

Already you will be transformed
into something other,
someone whose longing is only for more,
to be embraced again and again
by the invisible nameless who is there
to receive you,
to tell you that She is the one you desire.

You will not turn back.
There is no way down.

HOLY UNION

I do not know
who you are,
where you are from,
what you look like.

Yet I know
that when you arrive,
I once more know the secret,
holy marriage,
sacred union,
you and I are the same.

Then it is as though the vows
are renewed once more,
as if we have never been apart.

They talk of oneness,
abundance of connection,
sun and sunlight,
sea and wave,
air and breath,
always one.

THE BELOVED SHARES HER SECRET

I can't help it.
I keep on wondering
who you are,
why you keep coming,
how you are connected to me.

I think of a face, invisible
and smiling.

And then a voice says,
"Of course, you know me.
How could you not?
I am you and I have
never left."

"When you eat,
I am the taste
of the food you swallow.
When you hear music,
I send thrills of joy
through your body.
When you sleep,
I manufacture your dreams.

When you write,
you speak with my tongue.

Know that I love you,
for you are mine,
crafted from the same essence,
made of the same substance,
flame and burning candle,
always one."

THE SOLITARY ECSTATIC

Don't surrender your loneliness
so quickly.
Hafiz

Hafiz, do you know what it is
to be utterly, totally alone?

To be visited again and again
by those elements
that some call God
and still no friend
to share with, tell what is happening?

No one near
to hear your story
extend a welcoming hand?

Sometimes even God
is not enough.
Sometimes the loneliness
and something called rapture
are all you have.

SEEDS

We are all sent down here alone.
It is as if someone had
flung seeds from a higher place
and we came forth, blossoming
and seeking light.

Some of us took refuge
in already established forms,
ways of being.

We poured easily into pre-established molds.
We did not question, but accepted what was given,
glad for the comfort of beings of our kind.
Others of us were restless,
wanted answers,
rummaged ancient texts,
challenged teachers,
sought to remember,
where we came from,
our assignment here.

No one had an easy path.
Some were seduced by riches and success,
custom, their own talent.
Others forged ahead on
their own way,
a difficult journey,

no companions,
often no landmarks,
only savage sun,
blinding snow.

Our progress varied.
Those who did not travel
very far
were often happy just where they were
and had no desire to explore.
They chose not to ask too many questions
and took for granted what was given.
Others kept trying new pathways,
different routes and investigations
to move ahead.

And when these finally seemed
to arrive
at a longed for destination,
a different vision,
the rest were often suspicious,
felt indeed that they had
lost their way, needed help
or censure.

Nonetheless the adventurers
stood by their choices,
gave thanks to find at last
the hidden jewel
and knelt before what they knew
was holy,
the reason why they came.

BODHIDHARMA

They gave me a name
I did not understand.

It was that of a great figure,
someone written about in books,
known to history.
He was the one
who carried the dharma
to other countries,
made them his.

Sometimes I wonder
if I could be he,
shrunken and circumscribed,
struggling to remember,
to fulfill.

What if I were that one,
come back again,
trying to recall?
What would I do then?

What I Must Do

I have gone through the stages.
I have felt the extremes of joy and pain.
Flowers have spoken to me.
Trees have held me in their arms.
The Beloved has come often,
often unannounced.
Music has inhabited
my soul.

Now I wonder what I must do next.
Perhaps just this,
speaking to whoever
wishes to hear.

When I had my original awakening experience, I was given the new name of "Bodhidharma." I did not know what a "Bodhidharma" was, so I looked this word up and found that he was an ancient world teacher who took Buddhism to China. I did not dare to believe I was an incarnation of that great being but rather thought that perhaps I was named after him. I translated his name to mean "truth speaker" and so he was. And I have tried to be such in my own life through writing and speaking.

THE VISITOR

A knock came at the door.
"Who is it?" I cried.
"It is the Friend," said a voice.
"Go away," I shouted.
"I don't have a friend."

Next day, another knock came at my door.
"Who is it?" I demanded.
"It is the Friend," repeated the voice.
"Go away," I ordered.
"I don't have a friend."

On the next day, the knock came again.
This time, I decided to peer
through the window
to see who was making such a racket.

And then I saw myself standing there,
waiting to come in.

SUDDEN TURNS

I want to live my life all over again, to begin again,
to be utterly wild.
Mary Oliver

Do you want to live your life again,
to let that wild thing inside you
have its way this time,
to not hold back when the invitation
came on the silver platter,
the one which would have changed
your life forever?

Do you wish you had stood up
and said your truth
in a louder voice
even when the others didn't want to hear
what you were saying?
Do you wish you had told them
how wrong they were,
how they didn't understand?

Do you wish you had picked up
and moved to the mountains,
even if the snow blocked the door
in winter and the streams froze over,
and gone swimming naked in the pond
that summer with the stranger
who stopped by,

or hitchhiked through Greece with
a backpack and a smile?

Would you give up all the things
you did in exchange for what you refused,
surrender all those treasures in your
memory box,
the times when you were,
in fact,
quietly, suddenly wild,
took the unexpected turns in the path
which brought you here,
the place you are now,
this life you love
and would not trade.

THE ONE KISS

We claim to know things
but what we know
can be written on a fingernail.

Sages and savants
issue their proclamations,
but we move always
through a murky cloud
with an uncertain light at the center.

The center is what we call God.
We keep on circling and circling
yet we never arrive
at that final point.

But we know
that we move ever closer
to that place of mystery,
even if we cannot locate it
with precision.

But when the Beloved arrives
we no longer care
who wins the arguments,
whose theory is correct.
All we want is the single kiss
that makes us one.

BUDDHA'S FLOWER

I know about Buddha's flower,
emblem of truth.

But then there was that man
hanging from a tree,
the one who cried aloud
at the end.

How can I know both,
reconcile these disparities,
untangle good from evil?

Many have tried and failed.
Others choose to ignore the question.

I have no answers,
must for now just listen to this Beethoven and Bach,
behold the snow falling like white spring blossoms
outside my window
from the infinite to no where,
drift into rapture again.

Who am I to know final wisdom?
What I know is feeling in the heart,
spasms of joy,
the Beloved come once more.

Always

for the Beloved Within

Always, this is the thing
we hope for,
the desire we hold dear:

"Only a glimpse,"
we say,
"a taste,
a brief swallow . . ."
And thus we will be sated,
brought to the fountain
where the water ever flows,
the fire sweeps us
into a new composition,
and we are satisfied at last . . .

even as the light
brightens around us,
even as the music plays
sweeter
within.

In My House of Flesh

When you first arrived,
I did not recognize you.
You gave me a name
but I did not know
what it meant.

Gradually, we came
to know one another.
Your constant presence
brought me into
another awareness,
a different spectrum
of being.

Now I am easy
living with you in my house
of flesh,
finding you in daylight
playing over the
flowers outside
my window,
or coming in
with the evening breeze.

At night your perfume
enters,
surrounds me like
a lover come home.
Over and over
you whisper the syllables
of who you are
in my ear.
I still cannot hear the words clearly.
I no longer care.

OH, SEEKER

Oh, seeker, do not follow
the trodden ways
that the elders have created.
Too often these are deceptive,
have lost their luster.

Find your own pathway,
and you will arrive
at your true destination.

Nothing will be gained
by mindlessly repeating
ancient formulas
and doing prescribed practices
with little understanding.

Accept what rings true
but test each in the fire
of your own intelligence.

THE TRUE GUIDE

Do not
listen to those
who wear robes
and thus claim authority
or wish you to bow down.

There is an authority
higher than any of those
who demand blind obedience
and impose obligations.

Your true guide is the one
who lives within,
who will lead you
to the prize you yearn for,
the hidden jewel in your heart.

NO ENTRANCE FEE

In order to get
to this place
I am telling you about,
you do not have to pay
an entrance fee or
enroll in a course.

There will be no
official
directing traffic
or multiple signs
telling you which
way to go.

You will not have
to purchase
a fancy meditation cushion
or an expensive mala
to protect you from evil.

You will however
have to kneel down
and open your heart
and let the light
flood in.

If you are no longer
able to kneel,
then let your mind
go there.
There will be
plenty of light
to go around
and you will
get your share.

You will then know for certain
that you are loved
and there is
no price tag
on who you are.

THE UNSEEN POET

I am a fountain
pouring forth verses
that are seeking beauty.

I am a flower
opening into its own joy.

I am a shuttle
weaving a tapestry of words.

I am a mind that has
fallen in love with itself,
that wants to speak things
unheard of,
hidden for too long.

I am a map
marking with a circle
my heart's destination.

I am another,
a reality come
to be birthed
again and again.

QUESTION

Am I a falcon, a storm, or a strong song?
Rilke

Am I a flower, a tempest arriving,
or a wave dashing against the rocks?

Or perhaps a garden,
a forest path,
a mountain stream flowing
downward toward its
intended end?

Am I the drop that fell
into the ocean,
the child that cried aloud,
the jungle beast
seeking its prey?

The snow that hushed
the landscape,
the moon that silvered the earth,
the air that filtered the honey sun?

Am I a fading echo,
the music that
flooded the veins,
the scent of the rose unfolding?

Am I all these and more?
Abundance of being,
plethora of selves,
eternity of becoming.

TONIGHT

Tonight is the night
I have been waiting for.

The moon rising
has turned the world into
a floating seascape.

Light swims between the trees,
as if all things rested at the bottom
of an ocean of endless radiance.

Soon I will sleep
and dream that I inhabit
that other unworldly world.

Voices will speak to me,
whispering forgotten truths.

I will nod and smile and say,
"I know, I know."

THE ANCIENT SAINT REFLECTS

I have repented and prayed
through the dark night.

I have offered comfort and coins
to those who suffer,
are hungry and are not fed.

I have given all that I
once owned
to others,
that they might live.

Yet even now
I hear the sobs and exultant cries
of those who are ravaged
by incessant war
or are predators of many kinds,
those who cannot contain
the violence within
the love they feel.

What can I do
to abate these ills?
What can I give
to bring peace
to the hearts of all?

I must be quiet
and listen,
bring compassion to the world
wherever I can,
know that the Invisible One
is there, beside me always.

THE MYTHOLOGIZED SAINT SPEAKS

Frankly, at this point
I am not sure
whether I existed
or not.

I was someone who lived alone,
prayed a lot,
made friends with the birds
and the other animals.

Once at midnight an angel came
into my room,
filled everything with light.

After that I was no stranger
to rapture.

After I died
the stories began to be passed around,
miracles in places I had
never heard of,
healings of people I never knew.

They wrote about me
in books,
put up statues and paintings
in holy places

where people knelt
in awe.

I miss the trees
and the birds.
They were with me then
and even now
I sometimes hear them singing nearby
when I sleep.

BLESSING

for Patricia

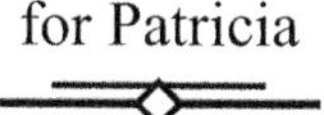

May the light of your soul
lead you ever forward
into new vistas,
novel experiences,
as you travel deeper
into the heart
of the mystic rose.

May it unfold
within your own chest
as you move always
toward the center
of final mystery.

May the Invisible One
who guides you
show you ever
the way to go,
as you travel forward
on the journey that never ends,
for knowledge of divinity is
the blessing
of those willing
to open to the delight
of union with the Beloved,
the Unseen Within.

May Beauty and Peace
be yours with each step you take
to become your true self,
the one you have always been.

THE AWAKENED ONE'S DILEMMA

What should I do?
I have known ecstasy.
I have been held close
to the beating heart of God.

The Mother has entered
my body, the veins,
carried me to other realms.

Who should I tell of this?
Who would be my confidante?

Always, there is mystery.
Never are there right words.
My tongue is held down
by a ribbon of love.

KUNDALINI, THE BELOVED WITHIN

Like any lover,
You can be wild or gentle.

You can arrive
like a tornado
roaring across the plains,
the funnel
Your forewarning.

Then Shiva dances
in our bodies,
our flesh quivers
in delight and we wonder
how much joy we can withstand,
whether we will survive.

Again,
You may arrive
like Buddha facing
his disciples,
holding up the flower in silence,
as if to proclaim,
"See, here it is,
the revelation you are seeking,
the final truth that lives everywhere."

KUNDALINI SPEAKS

Yes, I was the music
of your body.
I was the unstruck sound,
the holy syllable of your soul.

I floated through you
like one cloud
sharing its gold
with another.

I touched you in
the secret places
that only true lovers
know.

I awakened your heart
to what you had
no name for.

Was it the music of the spheres
stepped down so that you
could listen?
My soft vibrations
wafted through you
like the aftertones
of a chant
reverberating in
the rafters of a cathedral.

SINGERS

Oh, let the heart be opened
and expanded to its full:
let it be loved and give love
in full measure,
not wondering about
the why of it all.

Let this town that I love
not be ruined
by wrong vibrations.

Let this world that I love
not be destroyed
by those whose hearts
are frozen.

Outside my window.
there is a bird that sings.

It sings and sings,
no matter the weather,
the unstable barometer,
even after snow.

Let me be the same,
singing always,
and sometimes dancing a turn or two
to my song.

Passing overhead
there is a gathering of angels,
moving together as a single cloud.

When it is my turn to go,
may I join them,
this chorus of love,
even with my unsteady voice,
my uncertain ear,
echoes filling the vastness above,
the radiance below.

WHATEVER ELSE

Whatever else you do,
keep on climbing.
You know there is a mountain peak
up there, even if it is sometimes
covered in clouds,
even if the path is narrow
and often rutted, or covered in rocks.

Don't sprawl on a log
and count your sorrows,
or the betrayals that still haunt you.

Take out your favorite poems,
sing your own particular song,
the one that soothes you.
Think of your friends
who have given you courage
and sustenance along the way.

Send a little prayer
out to the universe.

They say everything is perfect, just as it is.

Make it happen that way.

There is lots of love
to go around.

THINKING AHEAD

I have already begun to say goodbye
to the things
I have loved on this earth,
in my life.

Something has told me
I may not live forever
after all,
may not survive to see
the next ruler installed,
the next country give way
whether or not
the distant "others" come.

Mostly, I think
it will be my friends I shall miss,
and though many will arrive
to join me soon enough,
some having already gone ahead
through the invisible gate.

I am told there are gardens
filled with exquisite flowers
and trees there,
colors you cannot imagine,
scents, sounds, abundance of love.

I am hoping I won't be asked
to solve the problems
I left hanging behind
when I departed,
won't have to remember
and try to erase
the memory of things
I did wrong,
how I misjudged some,
overrated others.

We will all be transfigured
in one way or another,
perhaps unrecognizable
balls of light,
flickering shadows
of fires in the distance,
awareness without form.

I trust there will be
plenty of Mozart and Bach
for those who ask,
that the vibrations we have tasted
here now and again,
will thrill through us
and we will become these again.

Mostly I fear
the loss of all that has
been me

in this lifetime,
like a book
whose print
has faded,
Table of Contents gone.

I would like to visit,
from time to time,
the "person" I was,
the being that was crafted
out of my flesh and blood,
however temporary
on the scene.

In the meantime,
I am hoping
for a new assignment,
some way to volunteer
to aid in what is going on
on my old planet,
my former home,
a place where joy
and tender feelings
still survive.

THE WEDDING NIGHT

When Rumi died
he called it his "wedding night."

I also hope
that I will at last be joined
to that larger self
I have been struggling to become
for so long.

Indeed, we have celebrated together
many times over,
love pouring
from one to another
in a rite of sacramental union.

In that other place
I will look back
with curiosity
and compassion
on who I was before,
who I am now,
the connection
between them,
the previous formulation
and the transfigured self.

At the Temple Gates

Some hover around outside,
linger at the portal,
never venture
within.

I don't blame them.
It's nicer,
safer out there.
Always longing,
never viewing the daemon
face to face,
hide and seek with the soul.

Never going in,
climbing up
on the altar
as the invisible one raises
his hand to
dismantle who you are.

Once there,
your parts have been torched and now
are unrecognizable.

Until they somehow join together
once again, in a new configuration.

OUR BEGINNING

It is never easy,
this moving ahead,
this coming to the place
where you and the Other
are one.

You have come here
in the way
that you are.

You will leave
much the same,
not wearing wigs
and false robes,
nor assuming the guise
of all your past accomplishments
but rather in the primal innocence
of what has always been you,
the hallmark
of your special being,
even as now
the wind speaks its secrets,
howling down the mountain
passes,
the rain making its way
into our hearts,
as we strain

to grasp
what is being said,
to hear the message
hidden in the
tight bud unfolding,
the cloud passing overhead
into the violet sun,
all fading in silence
and somewhere a whisper:

This is your beloved
arriving to embrace you
in a final recognition.
Be silent and attend.

CLIMBERS

I know what you want.

Something that speaks to you
just where you are.

As if this plateau you are on
was the only place
you were ever going to be,
the proper station
for one of your attainments.

Listen, my darling,
there are peaks and mountain heights
up ahead.

We are all climbing to the next level,
using the equipment
we have brought with us.

Don't stop.
Don't imagine you can now rest,
take a nap,
or check your messages.

Or hang around on the cliff face,
dangling in space,
hoping somebody will find you
and pull you up
while your ropes hold.

This is not a dress rehearsal.
It is your own scenario,
the one you wrote and are writing
even now, even this very day.

PAST LIFE

How can you know
who you were before?

Someone sent here
with an assignment
that you said *yes* to?
If so, what was it,
where is the document,
the agreement
with the map attached
to give you a guide?

A larger being,
now shrunk down
to human size,
just
to be reminded
of the difficulties of this plane,
how it is to be a mere member
of this particular species,
no one special?

Are you now someone waiting to be
kissed again by the spirit
reflected once more

in the wavering image
in your mirror?

Like a dream
that always disappears
around the corner of your mind
at the moment of
waking,
leaving behind only
vague images dissolving in air,
vanishing symbols and faces,
tiny clues
of what it might have been?

NATARAJA

for Brenda McMorrow

I called on you
hardly knowing who you were.
Something streamed through my body
and tore my previous self to shreds.

You then danced in my blood,
moved as light through my veins.

Now you were husband
to my thought,
master of who I was.

All I could say
was *yes, I am yours,*
do not leave.

Then I began to dance
in your footsteps.

Om nama Shivaya,
Om, Om, Om.

SUDDEN INSIGHTS

Sudden insights,
bursts of knowing--
where are they from?

Conclusive theories,
whole symphonies
arriving intact,
Einstein, Mozart,
you know the list.

Some say aliens arriving from other
planets,
some say from the *termas,*
texts or objects
hidden in rocks or earth or wood,
else embedded
in the psyche
even before birth,
now brought into the light,

What if such awareness rests
in all of us always,
ready to be discovered,
longing to be known?

What if we too
can access everything,
ready to be retrieved
like a safe of jewels
waiting for the right combination.

What would we do
with this immense revelation?
Would we simply vanish
in a flash?
How would we ever remember
the being who is us?

In the Tibetan Buddhist tradition, termas *are hidden teachings preserved in certain locations in nature or infused into the psyches of future masters,* tertons, *who will unveil them at the proper moment in history.*

THE TRAVELER

This is not merely
a journey
of the senses.

There are no landmarks,
no postcards and souvenirs
along the way.

It is a journey into
the cave of solitude.

You will enter realms
not on any map.

Your compass will fail,
and your vision will falter.

Even the stars, those
ancient guiding beacons,
will grow dim.

You will be
your own guide,
feeling your way forward
by the light of your own illumination.

Finally you will realize
you have been here before.

You will have reached
the center of your own being.

You will enter once more
through a door named
Love.

THE UNREPENTANT

You were born into a world
that had already decided
who you would be.

You were given
rituals, ceremonies,
explanations,
beliefs.

All directed
to moulding you into the right form,
an acceptable member
of the all.

Sometimes it was gatherings
in the desert or forest,
sometimes arrangements in pews.

Everyone agreed
that these were sanctioned
ways of being.
teachings of infallible meaning.

One day you walked
out of the forest,
fled the church,
looking for truth.

The others were not happy
with your behavior,
threatened you with
expulsion,
exile into
the outer darkness.

That did not deter you.
You did it anyway.
You became who you were.

A Mandala

Think of it
as a mandala,
with a sun in
its center.

There are a thousand portals,
all leading the way in.

Choose the opening
that suits you best,
whatever you name it.

Even a church can be
an entry.

Or study the paths,
ways of transforming
dross to gold,
cauldrons of change.

If you will let the Beloved
kiss you,
she will take you there
quickest of all.

POETS

Some got famous,
traveled,
signed books,
went on the internet,
collected royalties,
got prizes.

They were good.
They deserved it.
They worked hard
for their fame.

Others worked in darkness,
shared with a few friends
and neighbors,
got talked about locally,
even written up by the
town newspaper.

They never got rich from their offerings,
but thought of Emily
And her hidden verses,
Or Yeats with his one
good suit,
Whitman who printed his own books,

Blake (whose wife
put an empty plate before him
to remind him that the cupboard was bare)
I could go on,
the list is endless.

But they did not mind.
Oh, well, they thought,
what does it matter?
How much did Rumi charge?

ADVICE FOR GOING ON

Think of someone you adore,
say Mary Oliver or Denise Levertov
or, of course,
Rumi, the master of all.

Consider where their
connections came from,
somewhere invisible.
never on any map,
the lonely attic or desk,
the hours spent there
the striving for perfection
even when the ears had failed
or the pen could hardly be
held in the hand.

What was it
that kept them going,
even when all else
faded,
even when no one noticed?

Would you be willing
to give your life to this?

To forge ahead,
no matter what,
as the roses sang to you
along the garden paths,
as you danced
to the music
that only you heard?

THE MIRROR

Believe me,
it is still there.

That place inside,
where you have visited,
and sometimes lost your way.

You know how to get there,
the signs and sounds
that take you close.
They are still there too,
waiting for you to take notice.

When you arrive,
there will be a mirror.
It will not be just the same as the last time.
You will have changed,
improved, gotten better, wiser.

This time you will
not forget.
You will know what to do,
find your way quickly,
claim the image
looking back at you, the true yourself,
ready to begin again.

Ancient Allegories Revisited: The Soul Awakens

CINDERELLA: THE REBIRTH

There we were,
Cinderella among the ashes,
waiting, hoping, what could happen?

And what came over us
was not a dream
nor yet a reality, a mist, a veil,
a transfiguration
into something else.

As if the hidden one
had waved her wand,
as if we were no longer who we were,
not recognizable
yet always known.

Now we must wonder
are we dead or alive,
still flesh
walking among
the other fleshly beings,
some other new,
unforeseen essence,
some yet unnamed
self.

SLEEPING BEAUTY

Believe me,
it was not the prince
who waked her.
That fellow with
his eager lips,
his grasping hands.

Oh, no,
nothing of it was his,
it was rather a feeling,
a realization,
call it an awakening
inside
or the embrace
of an unseen lover.

And then a revelation
occurred,
she threw away
the old version
of who she had been
and knew, finally
and forever,
that she was who she was,
not the blurred mirror image,
but the real being,

the one ready to walk forth
and finally be seen,
as the ray of a star fell down
and lit up where she was
and some kind of triumphal music
played nearby.

3. ROMEO AND JULIET

Think of it as a metaphor,
an allegory of the soul.

First your spirit is drawn
to what is attractive,
but not permanent.

Then you encounter
the real thing,
the Beloved who
is also seeking you,
waiting to bestow
the secret embraces you long for.

First there is the love night,
the darkness in which you consecrate
your union,
and know that it will last always.

Then the fatal interruption,
something that drives you
away from one another,
not your doing
but fate, it would seem.
What have you done wrong?

Finally reunited, you must die
in one another's arms,
too late for return,
now you are something other,
like new beings ascending,
hybrids made of light and clay.

"Romeo and Juliet" traces the stages of the mystical journey. First there is the discovery of the false teaching, the wrong path for you. (Romeo infatuated with Rosalind at the ball.) Then there is the finding of the Beloved Herself, the goddess within, and the celebration of the love night. (Romeo and Juliet fall in love and spend the night together.) Next is the "dark night of the soul" when it feels that the connection with the divine is somehow lost, as if one is not worthy of the holy marriage. (The death experience in the tomb.) Then comes the final stage of rebirth, when you and the Beloved are One, "hybrids made of light and clay." Transcendence, rebirth growing out of death, either in this life or after, are not included in the play but are the culmination of the mystical path.

4. REMEMBERING NARCISSUS

Remember Narcissus?
How he fell in love
with his own image
and leapt into the water
to join his beloved?

Always we are striving
to merge with the ideal,
the perfect one beckoning
from the not quite seen.

Like two images
in the antique cameras
that had to merge
to obtain right focus.

We wonder which we are--
self or reflection,
flesh or image?

I think that all of us are striving to become the ideal self that we would like to be. Yet always we are called back, reminded that we are "merely human," with all our faults and failings there to confront us. But we do not give up. We keep the image before us calling us on to be one with the spirit we carry within.

NADA BRAHMA

Scientists have only recently learned that the particles of an oxygen atom vibrate in a major key and that blades of grass "sing."
Amazon review

In the forest
there was a note
and then an echo.

The unseen listener
heard,
an invisible music
played.

What shimmered
through the trees
had no beginning
or measurable source.

Yet it was everywhere,
celestial tones,
the unstruck sound,
nada brahma,
the beginning

Scientists today realize everything that exists is energy in movement or vibration, and that each vibration has its own sound, color, and visual pattern. When the vibration is slow enough we perceive it as our material world.

Nada *is a Sanskrit term for sound.* Brahma *is the name of God. Thus Nada Brahma is the sound of God or God is Sound.*

Rilke in Glory

Ah, Rainer Maria Rilke,
dreamer, poet,
lover of angels--

Who spoke those words
into your mouth?

Who held you
as you penned
these lines?

Was it the wind whistling
through the curtains
speaking in a language
that only you
understood?

Was it the mountain stream
imparting secrets
as it dashed over the rocks
toward
its unfathomed
destination?

What honey
fell into your throat

as you silently
listened?

Who holds you now
in angelic arms
as you sing your way
through still unmapped
regions,
unexplored territories
of the mind?

This poem was written after reading Rilke's majestic "Buddha *in Glory."*

When I Return

When I leave
I will become
Buddha again.

My face, my arms, my body--
all will glow
with quivering light.

I will sit quietly,
enjoying the bliss,
send rays of healing
in answer to prayers.

I will return,
the way the raindrop
falls
into the ocean
and becomes one with
the pounding surf,
the quiet pool.

If you want to see me,
you can look everywhere,
even in the paintings
and the sculptured forms.

I am the cloud passing,
the light
streaming through the forest.

I am the child crying,
the animal struggling in the trap.

I am this and all else,
I am that I am.

SANSKRIT SYLLABLES

Each sound of the Sanskrit alphabet has a corresponding vibration in our body. . . . Each sound then triggers an impulse within the body.
Linda Madani

Body a sounding board,
Vessel of rapture.

Frequencies of bliss
quivering in joy.

Always, it is as though
I am on the verge
of something,
a secret about to be unveiled,
a code designed
to unlock a key.

Always, it is this mystery,
a violin trying
to speak,
a flower trying to sing
in this dreaming universe.

These sounds press
toward knowings,
meanings

lost over centuries,
revelations carved
in the blood.

SANSKRIT CHANTED BY A SWAMI

They wear
their beards
and turbans,
darkened skins.

My face
is naked,
my head
unbound.

They speak
in strong deep
voices,
this language
is theirs.

I listen intently, understand
nothing,
yet Shiva/Shakti
are at play
in my body,
pulsations of delight.

I am one
with whatever
this is.

DREAMERS BENEATH THE QUILTS

I can't think, really,
how far we have come
on this road.

Maybe we have travelled
nowhere,
maybe we are still in the same
place
from which we started,
dreamers beneath the quilts,
imagining they are on a journey.

Yet, how beautiful it has been,
ripe sunsets,
snow quieting the hills,
stunning silences of midnight joy,
yourself awake and yawning,
what an astonishing dream
we have had,
wondering
who sent it down,
how it was conceived,
addressing thanks now
"to whom it may concern."

THE GOD PARTICLE

They call it
the God Particle.

After years of effort,
they finally trapped it,
the one they were looking for
that holds everything
together.

Finally, the puzzle was solved.

They found it
by whirling tiny bits
of things, not matter,
around in a huge,
expensive machine.
At last, they knew
everything,
had caught it
like an animal,
a wolf
or a bear trapped in a device.

Meantime a little girl in India
was dancing in joy.

She sighed as
she felt something within,
something she did not really
have a word for.
She named it "bliss,"
and she announced as
she twirled,
"See, I am feeling
the god within,
like a wee something circulating
in my blood,
like whatever it is
that holds the world together,
I call it Love."

QUESTIONS

Still, no matter how many times
I tell myself
that things will be all right,
that everything happens for the best,
that all is perfect just as it is,
some strange anxiety remains,
an inky beast lurking
at the bottom
of a dark well.

We can, of course,
hold hands and sing hymns
as the sinking ship goes down,
arrange the chairs
into a more orderly design.

Even though I have been informed
that all is going in the right direction,
that we are headed toward enveloping brightness,
the realm where issues no longer exist
and we are one with all that is,
still there is the feeling
that nothing is guaranteed,
things could go
one way or another
according to the whims

of the time,
that the rescuer will not
arrive as promised,
and dust will be the answer
to our prayers,
our supplications
to "whoever may be listening."

Yet, to be honest,
good things keep happening to me.
I have collected many years,
stored in a memory box
of all I have known,
find myself now
at the center of all I would yearn for,
friends a circle of love,
allowed to do
what I would most yearn to do,
things unfolding
the way they should.
Trust that I and the hidden world
are both headed
in the right direction.
Even kissed by the Goddess
now and again.

A STONE, A STAR

Sometimes blocked in, sometimes reaching out,
one moment your life is a stone in you, and the next, a star.
Rilke

Was it yesterday
that everything seemed
so futile?
The trees and flowers,
blossoming too early,
now covered in snow
at this Eastertide.
Ground lacquered
with threatening ice.
Will resurrection occur?

Yet today, a familiar sun.
Outside all luminous,
everything emerging
in clear definition
like a cleansed painting,
even the grass wearing
a fresh tunic of green,
the clouds regaining their lost shape,
no longer billowing blankets of grey
like sails spreading before a storm.

Even now I can feel things happening
underground,
incense is rising
as if from an invisible kiln
shaping a new world,
another new beginning.

TRANSFIGURATION

And now we approach
the keyhole,
the gap in the canyon of fate
where we go over the falls,
tumbling and thrashing
into the new world,
where we are fashioned
into an unfamiliar being,
someone who perpetually listens
to celestial tones
and is flooded
with constant bliss,
someone who can fly
or change form at will,
who constantly feels
God's breath on her face,
an essence transmuted.

We have been moving toward
this moment
for thousands of years,
alchemists in their laboratories,
cabalists hunched over their charts,
the Merkabah riders flying to heaven,
we too are flinging ourselves
over the edge,
into an unknown fate

TRICKS UP ITS SLEEVES

I think I lost sight of myself
years ago, when something happened
and I became someone other than what I was.

This new personage and I
are still getting acquainted.
It arrives with tricks up its flowing sleeves,
granting me new abilities,
unaccustomed gifts.

Now I can feel
beyond the range of feeling,
fall into fountains of rapture,
know more than
I can understand.

I do not know where all this
is taking me.

I no longer ask,
no longer care.

SOME OTHER PLACE

I am from some other place,
and I plan to go back there
when I die.
Rumi

Frankly, I am not sure
where I belong:
with the mystics
preparing to ascend,
some performing miracles
and speaking light language,
others listening to celestial music
playing within.

Or simply with the mavericks,
the ones who didn't fit in,
the strange ones
who went their own way
and persisted despite the objections
of everyone around.

Whatever category I belong to,
at least it was me,
following the role carved out
for me many ages ago in some other place,
a place I still get glimpses of now and again
and plan to return to after I leave.

How Will It Happen

Do not believe that
in order to ascend,
you must follow preset concepts,
worship certain images,
or perform specified rituals.

However, you must prepare by
entering
cauldrons of fire,
forests of bewilderment,
and meetings
with unknown figures
who appear in your path.

You must feel your way
blindly ahead through darkness and snow,
with no guide or savior
to sustain you,
to show you the way.

You will not be allowed
to measure your progress
until you reach the finish,
and by then, exhausted, hungry,
you may not realize
you have in fact arrived, that you have been there
all along.

DRINKING SONG

I will stay up late tonight
but I don't care
for I am drunk
on the wine of creation.

An unknown lover
holds my hand
and drinks with me
to all we don't know
amidst the shadow world
of today
and those still to come.

We care nothing
for the theories
and speculations,
the notions and combobulations.

What we know is this
feeling within,
this stream that flows
from somewhere to us,
making us like flowers
set aflame to drift
on transparent rivers
of joy.

THE TRANSFORMATION

Many had thought
it would be Wagnerian.
Lightening ripping the skies apart,
thunder leveling the hills.

They built deep shelters,
readied their private planes,
made reservations on whatever
might still move.

But when it came,
it was instead
a vast silence,
a stillness so overwhelming
that all were overtaken,
transfixed in awe.

The trains were now, literally,
stopped in their tracks,
the networks stood still,
the planes were frozen
in midair.
We ourselves could
no longer move or speak.

The cities too were submerged
in quiet
as the markets halted their chatter,
the subways ceased to run
and the cabs forgot
their destinations.

Then the throat of the earth
opened
and a single sound
came forth
in an unknown frequency,
an unfamiliar mode,
and we waited to see
if the angel would come.

Angels

Some looked up, saw an angel riding
earthward on a cloud,
and gasped.

Others saw nothing,
proclaimed the whole thing
a fraud,
mumbled that they ought
to pass laws.

Still others wandered aimlessly,
looking under rocks and trees
for answers,
sleepwalkers wishing that someone
would come along and find them.

The angel kept on coming
and soon was joined
by others of her kind,
all plunging down to earth
to help her in her need.

The alarm bell had sounded.
The sirens were going off.
The angels heard and were kissing awake
all who were ready, who were open.

When the Great Angel Came

Then the angel came,
she arrived in a halo of fire
so intense we hid our eyes.

Some dropped to their knees.
Others wept.

Then, although she spoke no words,
she gave us a message
that we all could comprehend.

She gave us truths
we had forgotten.
She reminded us of things
that we knew
but failed to practice.

For some, she quoted
from the holy books
they each revered.
For the rest, she gave old words
full of new meanings.

Finally, one of us
asked her name.

She paused, and then as she
swept away
(again in a blaze of fire)
she answered "Love"
and the sound echoed
through the heavens
and across the universe
before it became a full throated song
by the same name.

BECAUSE

Because I had no one to lead me . . .

Because I heard no voice
telling me how to go . . .

Because no book or article
was there to inform me . . .

I fled into myself
and there found
the treasure I was seeking.

A Delicate Rapture

The spirit seeks to be
ever more subtle.
It no longer comes
as a great storm,
thunder and flashes
of light,
nor a deluge flooding
the landscape.

It is now so soft
it cannot be described.
It floats gently over
your body,
root to crown,
wherever you put your mind.

Once you thought you had
reached your goal
when by merely moving
your eyes or hands,
you sent it here and there,
caressed by bliss.

Now nothing more is needed
but wishing it into place.

This is a process
that never ends,
always drawing you
closer to the one within,
to Love.

Who We Are

The I does not exist,
only God is real.
Rumi

We are particles
dancing in the bloodstream
of an unknown god.

We are cells
in the eye
of the One who sees all.

We are the rough dross
being refined into
the pure gold
of light, of love,
of Being.

THE HAPPENING

Frankly, I am getting a bit worried.
Earthquakes to the West,
blizzards attacking the East,
chaos at the top,
violence ripping the world apart
everywhere.

What have we done
to create such circumstance?
Are we now mere victims,
arms bound to our chests and tongues gagged,
waiting silently for what is next,
is there nothing we can do?

Yet, despite all,
there is a secret.
and it is telling us
that more is involved
than is described in the
newspapers
or talked about
by the panels of experts.
Something is afoot,
something strange and wonderful
and unseen.
And real.

It is sending out a signal
that many are receiving.
It is calling out in
an unnamed voice
that great numbers are
resonating with.

Call it Spirit,
call it Joy,
call it whatever you like,
it is here,
it is happening,
we are its progeny,
its children of love.

We are here
to proclaim its presence,
to allow its reality to happen
in our cells
and our veins,
to allow it to refashion us
into the next incarnation of who we are.

THE INITIATION

The purpose of life
is to embody the transcendent.
the Dalai Lama

Somehow we are found.
By some method we are discovered,
observed, finally given signals
that tell us (secretly) to prepare.

Even then
we are not ready.
How could we be?
We are taken from whatever place
in the world we occupy
and are suddenly shaped
into an unrecognizable being,
a stranger to ourselves
and others.
We are thrown
into rapture or perhaps even pain,
states we may not even
have names for.

Again and again the rapture permeates
our bodies.
It fills us with joy

day after day, year after year,
until finally we succumb totally
to that which it is,
its constant infusions
of bliss and compassionate love.

At last we no longer question
that we and it are one.
Have ever been
and always will be.
It is who we are,
the essential unsuspected
truth of our identity.
Its sensed presence
comes and goes
like that of any lover,
but we know
that seen or unseen,
it is always there.

We give it the names
of a god or goddess,
a spirit or a guide.
Some call it The Beloved.
Some call it God.

We accept in silence.
We bow our heads in awe.

We wait for the next unfolding.

THE TRANSITION

Even as the world around crumbles,
the gates of heaven
are opening.
Indeed angels
are flowing down
mingling among the crowds.

Their children are appearing
among us
with strange talents
we do not understand.

Something is carrying us
into another universe,
where colors deepen
and frequencies rise.

The old gods are wakening,
the times when the oracles spoke.

Some of us are hearing
unknown music of the sublime.
Others are seeing
images of holy ones, visions of the real.

No one can explain what
is happening.

We are now captives of rapture,
of seeing beyond the veils.

We must surrender to vastness,
to love.

We must become more
than we are.

About the Author

Dorothy Walters, Ph.D., spent most of her early professional life as a professor of English literature in various Midwestern universities. She helped to found one of the first women's studies programs in this country and served as the director of this program for many years. After an extended residence in San Francisco, she now lives and writes in Colorado, where she has a close relationship with the mountains as well as various streams and canyons.

She underwent a major Kundalini awakening in 1981, a phenomenon totally unfamiliar to her as well as to most of her contemporaries at the time. Since then she has devoted her life to researching and writing about this subject and to witnessing the unfolding of this process within herself as well as assisting others on a similar path through writing and other means. As someone who made her extensive journey without the direction of any external leader or guru, church or established order, she is a strong believer in the "guru within," the inner guide rather than the external authority figure or institution.

Walters feels that universal Kundalini awakening is the means for planetary and personal evolution of consciousness, and that evidence of planetary initiation is becoming more and more prevalent. Her Kundalini awakening and subsequent process of unfolding are described in her memoir *Unmasking the Rose, A Record of a Kundalini Initiation.* Her poems, which have been published in several volumes, included in anthologies and journals, have also been set to music and sung at the Royal Opera House in London and Harvard University, used as texts for sermons, included in doctoral projects and have given inspiration to many.

Dorothy Walters often gives counsel and referral free of charge to those undergoing spontaneous Kundalini awakening and spiritual transformation. You can find more of her work at: www.kundalinisplendor.blogspot.com

Printed in Great Britain
by Amazon

26494624R00109